Dedication
Dedication

This book is dedicated to my husband, Paul, who has had to put up with all the discussions on renewing the mind and having to read the book. Thank you for the support.

This is also dedicated to my Mom, Brenda and Dad, David, who are the ones that have instilled in my life many values and the love of books. Thanks

Thank you to the publishers of the Modern English Version Bible for the use of their translation.

Thank you to my sister, Tamlyn for helping me with the editing.

Forward

'Renewing the mind' is a clear and very practical discourse of 'How To'. It shows us simply and powerfully the What, Who, How and Why of Mind renewal by scripture not from a theological perspective but clearly from experiential knowledge of the successful application of scripture and its results which is the Holy Spirit manifestation of it is written.

This book further proves that mind renewal is not some far out of reach someday maybe but who knows the answer to prayer but shows the Word is near you, even in your heart and in your mouth.

This book takes away all doubt and liberates you to obedience to the Word of God empowering your will to responsibility so don't be hearers of the Word only deceiving yourself but be ye doers transformed by the renewing of your minds.

By Paul Murray
Renewing The Mind

The author has communicated the heart of God to the reader in a very clear, precise and correct way by not only being creative in explaining the content of the Bible chapters and verses, but also defying with consideration the reader's mind, in grasping, understanding and be willing to train one's mind to the Word of God, with guidelines on How to do it, When to do it, Where to do it, Why do it and much more beside.

In a nutshell, this book reveals, by God's Word, how to go about in the lifelong process of diligently renewing the human mind to the mind of Jesus Christ, so that as they do so, subsequently one becomes more like Him in thoughts, words and actions.

By Bonaventura Apicella

INDEX

Introduction

Renewing The Mind is every minute of every day for the rest of your Christian life. This will not only help you in your Christian walk with God but also help you to help others, some might be Christians, but most will be non-Christians.

Renewing The Mind plays an important role in our own lives because it makes us more attune to the Word of God and to His will for us so that we can have a normal Christian life and to help others.

Renewing The Mind will help us to discern the difference between true and false teachings that are being taught in the church, TV broadcasts, teaching tapes or CD'S and books that we read or listen to.

As you read this book I hope it will not only give you a reason to renew your mind but also to awaken you to the truths of the Bible so that you become Doers of the Word of God rather than just sitting in a church and doing nothing. There is more to being a Christian than just doing things in the church.

I pray that this book will give you the encouragement to be a Doer, and to grow in the Word of God and become more what we should be, and that is more like Jesus, do what Jesus did with the same power and authority.

Chapter 1

What Is Renewing The Mind

Renewing The Mind is the part we must do to get our minds on the Word of God. What is our mind? Our whole being is made up of three parts. The spirit, the soul and the body. The soul is our will and where all our thoughts and feelings come from. It's our intellect, it's where the knowledge we gain from by either reading, writing, doing or listing, is stored. In some ways it forms our nature. If you are born again, your spirit is the Holy Spirit so therefore we have the very nature of God already in us. Our minds or souls must be renewed to what the Spirit in us knows. This is the part where we renew our mind. God has already done what He is going to do, He gave us a new spirit and we have become a new creature.

2 Corinthians 5:17 (MEV).

17. "Therefore, if any man be in Christ, he is a new creature. Old things have passed away. Look, all thing have become new."

But our minds are still the same, we still think the same way as we did before we were born again. So, this is the part where we need to change.

This is the part we must renew. Renew means to make new. Our thinking and actions need to be made new.

Matthew 22:37 (MEV)

*37. "Jesus said to him, "You shall love the Lord your God with all your **heart**, and with all your **soul**, and with all your **mind**"*

The word heart is the Greek word kardia 'the heart, that is, (figuratively)the thoughts or feelings (mind); also (by analogy) the middle:-(+broken-) heart (-ed)'. (G2588)

The Greek word for soul is psuchē 'breath, that is (by implication) spirit, abstractly or concretely (the animal sentient principle only the rational and immortal soul; is mere vitality, even plants: these terms thus exactly correspond to the Hebrew words for heart (+- ily), life, mind, soul, +us, +you' and the word mind from the Greek is dianoia, which means ' deep thought, properly the faculty (mind or its disposition) by implication its exercise:-imagination, mind, understanding." (G5590)

The Greek word for mind is dianoia. 'Deep thought, properly the faculty (mind or its disposition), by implication its exercise: - imagination, mind, understanding.' (G1271)

From this we know that we are to love the Lord with all we have, which includes our minds.

Renewing our mind is to take what the Bible says, and to renovate our minds to it. It's like when we are renovating an old house. We first take out what should not be there, i.e. things that no longer work, rotten, or unsafe to use. Once this has been done, we replace it with new things, like cupboards, floors, and even change the color on the walls. This house is like our body and our souls are the things that are inside the house. As we renew our minds to the will of God, it's like us taking things and replacing them for new. This is what we are doing by replacing the things of the world that have come into our soulish realm, with the Word of God.

Chapter 2

Who Has To Renew Their Mind?

Romans 12:2 (MEV)

*2. "Do not be **conformed** to this world but be **transformed** by the renewing of your mind, that you may prove what is that good and acceptable and perfect will of God"*

We see here that God is saying that we are not to be conformed (G4964) fashioned alike, conform to the same pattern, fashion self-according) to what? The world, that is the world systems, ideologies etc.…

Who must be transformed by the renewing of the mind? Ye, meaning you and me, it is not God, or the Holy Spirit or Jesus, but us.

We are to do what? Transform in the Greek is metamorphoō. 'To transform (literally or figuratively "metamorphose"): -to change, transfigure, metamorphose.' (G3339)

What do we have to transform? Our mind. The word mind in the Greek is nous 'the intellect, that is; mind (divine or human, in thought, feeling, or will), by implication meaning: - mind understanding.' (G3563)

What do we renew our minds to? To what is that good, and acceptable and perfect the will of God.

From this scripture we see that it is us that must renew our mind to the will of God.

Ephesians 4:22-25 (MEV)

22.That you put off the former way of life in the old nature, which is corrupt according to the deceitful lusts, 23. and be renewed in the spirit of your mind; 24. And that you put on the new nature, which was created according to God in righteousness and true holiness. 25. Therefore, putting away lying, let every man speak truthfully with his neighbour, for we are member of one another.

Again, we see that we are to put off the old man and put on the new man. It is us that must renew the spirit of our minds. It's not God, your pastor, Jesus, Holy Spirit that does it, but you.

The Holy Spirit will lead you to all truth.

Romans 8:14-16 (MEV)

14. For as many as are led by the Spirit of God, these are the sons of God. 15. For you have not received the spirit of slavery again to fear. But you have received the Spirit of adoption, by whom we cry, "Abba, Father." 16. The Spirit Himself bears witness with our spirits that we are the children of God:

2 Corinthians 5:17 (MEV).

17. Therefore if any man is in Christ, he is a new creature. Old things have passed away. Look, all things are become new.

God has dealt with all sin in our lives and has placed a new spirit in us, that is the Holy Spirit. All that has already been done. But our soulish or fleshly, body and mind realm they need to be renewed. They are the ones that need to be crucified with Christ, they are the ones that need to die more and be replaced with Christ and as we do this we will find that we are becoming more powerful in our ministry to others because we begin to look more like Jesus.

We are not to be a dam where everything we receive only stops at us. We are to be rivers that as we receive, we give to others.

Matthew 10:7-8 (MEV)

7. And as you go, preach, saying, 'The Kingdom of heaven is at hand.' 8. Heal the sick, cleanse the lepers, raise the dead and cast out demons. Freely you have received, freely give.

As you renew your mind, you will need to not only hold onto what you have learned but also to give out what you have learned.

The more you renew your mind, the more you get an understanding of the will of God, the more you move in power, i.e. the more results you get when you are praying for the sick. It's not because you are getting more favor from God, but rather the fact that you have a better understanding of His will, and as you do the will of God the more experiential knowledge, you have, the more power you walk in. There is no place for doubt when you renew your mind to the Word of God.   It's because you have a better understanding and you are able to believe what your position is in Christ; you are able to stretch yourself more.

Chapter 3

How To Renew Our Mind?

To renew your mind, you first must have a choice as to what to renew your mind to. God's will or the world's view (Satan's view). So, as Believers we should be renewing our mind to the will of God. So, where do we find the will of God? Do we trust in our visions, angels, pastors, prophets, evangelists, teachers and apostles, or books or man's opinions to show us the will of God? Or do we turn to the Bible to find the will of God? Yes, the will of God is found in the Bible not in visions, teachings, pastors, books, evangelists etc.

As Paul says in Galatians, that if anyone, man or angels that does not preach the gospel of Jesus and we listen to those things then, we condemn ourselves. We become accursed.

Galatians 1:6-10 (MEV)

6. I marvel that you are turning away so soon from Him who called you in the grace of Christ to different gospel. 7. Which is not a gospel. But there are some who trouble you and would pervert the gospel of Christ. 8. Although if we or an angel from heaven preach any another gospel to you than the one we have preached to you, let him be accursed. 9. As we said before, so I say now again, If anyone preaches any other gospel to you than the one have received, let him be accursed.

We know we must read the Bible to get God's will.

The next question is how do we read the Bible?

Chapter 4

How To Read Your Bible?

Many of us have been in the church for a long time and have found that we have been taught things that are not correct. We tend to read the Bible as we are taught instead of reading every word.

To start off with, we need to choose a version of Bible that is accurate. I suggest that you get a hold of King James version, English Revised Version, a Young's Literal Version and or Wuest. A good Bible program like E-Sword that can be download free of charge has some of these versions. Also, you will need to have a Strong's Exhaustive Concordance with the Hebrew and Greek dictionaries. This will aid you in your studying the Bible. E-Sword has a Strong's Concordance attached to a King James Bible. These are tools to help you to get to the understanding more of the Bible so that you can do the Word, which is the meat of the Word.

Let's start with how to read the Bible. As I said before that often we read the Bible according to what we are taught. So we need to look at the Bible as if we have never seen or read or heard teachings on it before. This alone will open the Bible in a different way.

Let's take the well-known verse

John 3:16 (KJV)

"For God so loved the world, that he gave his only begotten Son, That whosoever believeth in him should not perish but have everlasting life."

Often, we miss the end bit where it says that whosoever, so who is whosoever? That is anyone, not just the unsaved but us as well.

1. We need to read each word. To do this we can read it out loud, so we are not only reading but we are hearing as well.

2. We can take a verse and read it repeatedly out loud emphasizing a different word each time. I.e. make a word louder than the other. Do this with each word in the verse.

Let's look at the same scripture John 3:16.

The words in bold is the words that you are emphasis or its louder than the other words.

John 3:16.

For God so loved the world, that he gave his only begotten Son, That whosoever believeth in him should not perish but have everlasting life

For **God** so loved the world, that he gave his only begotten Son, That whosoever believeth in him should not perish but have everlasting life."

For God **so** loved the world, that he gave his only begotten Son, That whosoever believeth in him should not perish but have everlasting life."

For God so **loved** the world, that he gave his only begotten Son, That whosoever believeth in him should not perish but have everlasting life."

For God so loved **the** world, that he gave his only begotten Son, That whosoever believeth in him should not perish but have everlasting life."

Do this for each word saying the scripture repeatedly till you get to the last word.

In this verse we have a total of 25 words, so we need to have said it 25 times.

This will help you to read the verse with all its words, so you don't miss any of the words. Also, it will help you to remember the verse and you might get a better understanding of the verse as well.

3. We need to read the scripture in context, i.e. read 7 verses above and below the verse you are reading.

This gives us the overview of what is been said, and what God is saying so it might be a good idea to read the chapters before and after. Then it might be a better idea and that is to read the whole book where that verse is. Often, we read the verses as they are placed, ignoring the punctuation marks that let us know that the sentence is complete. Some sentences in the Bible may go over a few verses so be aware of this and read it as a sentence than as a verse. Reading your Bible this way will help you to not read it according to the way you have been taught to read this verse.

4. Take notice of the small words like: all, whosoever, nothing, whatsoever and shall. As these words are often missed and not believed. E.g. nothing shall harm me. What can harm me? Nothing. That means if I step on a snake by accident and it bites me, that bite will not harm me.

5. Ask questions like who, where, when, how, why, what, and what now. These questions you can find the answers in the passage of scripture that you are reading. I.e. don't look for the answers to the questions that you have asked in john, in Genesis. I.e. using the verse John 3:16, let's ask the following questions.

1. Who loves the world?
2. What did He Give us?
3. Who can believe on Him?
4. What happens when we believe in him?
5. What is everlasting life?
6. What do I now do with this? Do I ignore this and carry on?
   Who do I begin to believe in, Jesus?

Make sure that your answers can go back to the Word of God. Always check your answers against the word of God.

I cannot stress enough how important it is that you make the Word of God your standard, your foundation stone. It's to become so real in your life that the car or table is not as real as the Word.

If you are going about saying "I don't know the will of God" or "God has something planned for me but I don't know what it is" then you are not reading your Bible. As in the Bible it's not only about God and Jesus and many of the good people in the Bible. But it also shows you the will of God. E.g.; does God love everyone, even sinners? Well according to John 3:16 He loved the world so much that He was willing to pay a sacrifice of His son, to die for us. Please note the scripture does not say He loved the Believers, but that He loved the world. So, God loves those that are believers, sinners, non-believers, murders, and everyone involved in different religions, including witchcraft, Satanists etc. Just because you are a believer does not make God love you more.

6. Use the Strong's Exhaustive Concordance or a Bible program like E-Sword to get what the different words mean in the original language. For example, the word loved in John 3:16 can mean more than just love like we might think of it as in todays modern language.

a. How to use a Strong's Exhaustive Concordance.
i. Look up the word in the concordance for example the word
   Love in John 3:16.
ii. You will see that there is a Greek number for the word. The
   Greek number for loved in John 3:16 is G25.
iii. Then go to the Greek dictionary at the back of the
   concordance or just click on the number if you are using the
   e-sword program and read what it means. So, loved in
   John 3:16 is the Greek word agapaō which means to love (in a
   social or moral sense): - (be-) love (-ed).

7. Read the same verse in a different version of the Bible. You
can read it in the King James (KJV), English Standard (ESV),
Young's Literal Translation (YLT) or the Wuest. Let's see the
different versions of John 3:16

For God so loved the world, that he gave his only begotten Son,
that whosoever believeth in him should not perish, but have
everlasting life. (KJV)

For God so loved the world, that he gave his only Son, that
whoever believes in him should not perish but have eternal life.
(ESV)

For God did so love the world, that His Son- the only begotten- He
gave, that everyone who is believing in him may not perish but
may have life age-during. (YLT)

For in such manner did God love the world, insomuch that His
Son, the uniquely begotten One, He gave in order that everyone
who places his trust in Him may not perish but may be having life
eternal. (Wuest)

You can see the differences and hopefully get a better
understanding of what you have read.

8. This is the most important step of all. You must DO the word that you have just read and studied. You must apply what you have read to your life. If you don't do the Word, then you are not experiencing the fullness of God, you are not acting as a Son of God but rather a son of man. If you don't do the Word, then you are like the foolish man who built his house upon the sand and when the storms come you are unable to stand.

Matthew 7:24-27 (MEV)

24. Whoever hears these sayings of Mine, and does them, I will liken him to a wise man, who built his house on a rock. 25. And the rain descended, the floods came, and the winds blew, and beat on that house. And it did not fall, for it was founded a rock. 26. And every one who hears these sayings of Mine and does not do them will be likened to a foolish man who built his house upon the sand. 27. And the rain descended, the floods came, and the winds blew, and beat on that house. And it fell. And its fall was great.

You see that we have to be both hearers and doers of God's Word. We see this through the New Testament.

Chapter 5

Declarations

What are declarations?

Declarations are verses from the Bible that you have taken and made them personal and you confesses them each day.

This will help you to not only memorize the scripture but also to renew your mind to the truth, that when you come under attack from the enemy you are standing strong.

So How Do We Turn Scripture Verses Into Declarations?

Let's take the Scripture below and turn it into a personal declaration.

Romans 8:9a (MEV)

"You, however, are not in the flesh but in the Spirit, if indeed the Spirit of God lives in you."

1. You need to replace the all the ye and you with your own name.

Romans 8:9a "But Megan are not in the flesh but in the Spirit, if so be that the Spirit of God dwell in Megan"

2. Now we turn it into daily confessions by breaking it down further. As you can see there is two parts to this portion of the scripture.

a) But Megan are not in the flesh but in the Spirit
b) If so be that the Spirit of God dwell in Megan.

3. Now turn each part into a declaration that makes sense.

a) I am not in the flesh but I am in the Spirit
b) I have the Spirit of God dwelling in Me, He never leaves me.

4. Write them out and you can then read them out loud each day. You could even record yourself doing them so, that you can copy them onto a disk and play them in the car.

Here are some other scriptures you can turn into declarations as practice using the steps above.

Romans 8:11 (MEV)

11. "But if the Spirit of Him who raised Jesus from the dead lives in you, He who raised Christ from the dead will also give life to your mortal bodies through His Spirit that lives in you."

Galatians 4:7 (MEV)

7. "Therefore you are no longer a servant, but a son, and if a son, then an heir of God through Christ."

Matthew 5:14 (MEV)

14. "You are the light of the world. A city that is set on a hill cannot be hidden."

Declarations also help you to meditate on the Word of God. The book of Psalms is full of instructions on meditating on the word of God.

Psalm 1:2 (MEV)

2."but his delight is in the law of the Lord, and in His law he **meditates** *day and night."*

The Greek word for meditate is hagah (G1897) which is to murmur (in pleasure or anger); by implication to ponder: - imagine, meditate, mourn, mutter, roar X sore, speak, study, talk, utter.

When we see the word meditate, we often think about sitting in the lotus position and saying hymmmm, this is not meditating at all. Meditate is to think about, picture, study and talk about what you have read in the Bible.

From Psalm 1:2 we are to meditate on God's law (which is to love the Lord your God, and to love your neighbour) day and night.

Psalm 63:6 (MEV)

6. "When I remember You on my bed, and meditate on You in the night watches,"

Again, we are to think and imagine on God when we are in bed about to rest.

Psalm 77:12

12. "I will meditate also on all Your work and ponder on Your mighty deeds." (MEV)

We need to think about all that God has done and to talk about what He has done. This brings to remembrance the scripture where it says in Revelation 12:11 "And they overcame him by the blood of the Lamb and the word of their testimony, and they loved not their lives unto the death." What is our testimony? Our testimony is what God has done in our lives, whether it be healings, finances, etc.....,

Here are other References for you to look up and study on meditating:

Psalm 119:5, Psalm 119:23, Psalm 119:48, Psalm 119:78, Psalm 119:148 and Psalm 143:5.

Chapter 6

Doubting

Doubting is when you begin to believe that the Word of God is not true. This can hinder your walk with God, and your ability to serve mankind.

Mark 11:22-23 (MEV)

*22. Jesus answered them, "Have faith in God. 23. For truly I say to you, whoever says to this mountain, 'Be removed and be thrown into the sea,' and does not **doubt** in his heart, but believes that what he says will come to pass, he will have whatever he says.*

The word doubt in Greek is diakrinô (G1252) From G1223 and G2919; to separate thoroughly, that is, (literally and reflexively) to withdraw from, or (by implication) oppose; figuratively to discriminate (by implication decide), or (reflexively) hesitate: - contend, make (to) differ (-ence), discern, doubt, judge, be partial, stagger, waver.

Doubt is a sin, because whatever is not of faith is sin.

Romans 14:23 (MEV)

*23. But he who **doubts** is condemned if he eats, because it is not from faith, for whatever is not from faith is sin.*

The Greek word for doubts is = to separate thoroughly, to withdraw from, oppose, to discriminate, hesitate, contend, to differ, discern, doubt, judge, be partial, stagger, to waver.

There is nothing that says our thoughts or what we think is doubt, but rather it's an action that we take on that thought.

When you are out shopping, and you see someone who is limping
and you say yes, there is someone I can pray for, then as you
start going up to pray for him, then you get the thought, "its not
going to work, you are just going to make a fool of yourself. If you
pray for him and he is not healed". ok now that is just a thought.
That thought is a temptation to doubt and not doubt.

James 1:14-15 (MEV)

*14. But each man is tempted when he is drawn away by his own
lust and enticed. 15. Then, when lust has conceived, it brings forth
sin; and when sin is finished, it brings forth death.*

Temptation is not sin, it's the doing of the temptation that is sin.
When we have a thought to doubt, we are not doubting. It's when
we walk away from doing what we were going to do is doubting.
I.e. praying for that person's healing is the sin.
You must make a choice whether you are going to act on that
thought or are you going to carry on and pray for that person.
When you have these thoughts, you have a choice, to a. Draw
back and sin, or B. Move forward into faith and life which is doing
God's word.

Where did this thought come from? It came from satan. The devil
is very sly, and cunning, as he will use enough truth for you to
accept it but also enough non-truths to make you err or sin. The
thought of not praying for someone is not sin, but when you act on
that thought it becomes sin, but the devil has told you that
because you had that thought of not believing that it would work,
then you have sinned already by doubting, then you don't act on it.

Let's take the shopping incident again, you are about to go up to
pray for the person and you get the thought "what if this does not
work?" right up till now you have not sinned, or doubted. If you
decided to say to your thought ok, I believe you and I won't go and
pray for that person and you walk away, you have sinned. But if
you decided to say to your thought, hang on in Mark 16:18 it says
They shall take up serpents, and if they drink any deadly thing,

 it shall not hurt them; they shall lay hands on the sick, and they shall recover. So, I tell my thought this. "When I lay hands on the sick they shall recover, so I am going to lay hands on the sick and they shall recover". This is walking on the word of God, this is doing the works of God. This is what the Bible says we are to do and this is the promise we have.

This principal can be used in everything we do. We need to take heed to what we think and take it captive and line it up with the word of God. This is also how we renew our minds.
How to put this into action:

1. Identify the thought
2. Determine if it lines up with the word of God. If it does not then decide not to believe it, and find one or more scripture that you can learn to believe in.

Example. The thought is: I can't do this (healing or whatever)

1. So we have identified what it is telling me that I can't do this
2. Does it line up with the word of God? No it does not! The word of God says, in

Philippians 4:13 (MEV)

13. "I can do all things because of Christ who strengthens me."

The next time that thought comes into your head you should say, "Hang on, I can do all things, because of Christ who is in me and I am in Him, and he strengthens me to do it."

Let's watch what we think as well as what we say, and line it up with the word of God.

To sum up. A thought is a temptation to doubt. Temptation only becomes a sin when we act on it. To have a thought of doubt is not a sin, but it's when we act on that thought it becomes doubt, and doubt is a sin

Chapter 7

Being Doers Of The Word

We now know how to read and study our Bible, and about meditating on what we have learnt. Now the next step is What Now? What do we do with the information that we have learnt? Do we just put it down to learning? Or do we act on it. If we are to just put it down to learning something, it's like us reading and studying a recipe for chocolate cake. We can know how to make it, what ingredients we need, and how long it is to bake, but unless we do the baking, we will never have that chocolate cake to eat.

This is the same with the Word of God. We can study the Bible and be able to read it in its original languages, but we would not get the experiences of God's goodness to us and those we encounter as we do the Word, unless we act on what we have learnt. We will not have any testimonies to overcome the enemy. People will argue with you about what the Bible says, but they cannot argue with you about your testimonies or results when you have prayed or healed people.

Let's look at what Jesus said about doing the Word of God.

Matthew 7:21-23 (MEV)

21. "Not everyone who says to Me, 'Lord, Lord,' shall enter the kingdom of heaven, but he who does the will of My Father who is in heaven. 22. Many will say to Me on that day, 'Lord, Lord, have we not prophesied in Your name, cast out demons in Your name, and done many wonderful works in Your name?' 23. But then I will declare to them, 'I never knew you. Depart from Me, you who practice evil.

Jesus is saying that not everyone who calls Him Lord will enter into the Kingdom of heaven. If many people believe that they are going to enter the Kingdom of Heaven by just going to church on a Sunday and any midweek meeting or even those that regularly study the Bible, they won't get to enter the Kingdom of heaven. Even those that we think are doing the Word, will not be recognized by Jesus.   Why? Well He tells you why, because they have not been doing what they have learnt. They are doing some of the things but not all of Jesus sayings. Or they have done these things so that they can be famous or well known, or even selling the power of God to gain money which is all done in the name of Jesus. This portion of scripture comes before the parable of the wise man and the foolish man. Why have we separated this from what Jesus says next?

Matthew 7:24- 27 (MEV)

24. "Whoever hears these sayings of Mine and does them, I will liken him to a wise man who built his house on a rock. 25. And the rain descended, the floods came, and the winds blew and beat on that house. And it did not fall, for it was founded a rock.
26. And every one who hears these sayings of Mine and does not do them will be likened to a foolish man who built his house on the sand. 27. And the rain descended, the floods came, and the winds blew and beat on that house. And it fell. And its fall was great."

How many of us have heard people teaching that the wise man was the man who became born-again and the foolish man was the unbeliever? Well let's take note of the first 9 words in verse 24, "Whoever hears these sayings of Mine and does them," So if we can see that it's those who believe as they have heard the sayings of Jesus, as Jesus is talking, and those that does them, is a wise man. We can conclude that we can hear Jesus sayings and do them then we are a wise man who is set firmly on the Word of God that when troubles come his way (which they will because of the enemy) then he will not fall.

In verse 26, let's look at the first 14 words, "And every one who hears these sayings of Mine and does not do them" So if you believe and do not do what Jesus has said you are to do, then you are a foolish man. So how many of us do not do what Jesus has asked us to do. Many have used the excuse that they are waiting for God to tell them what to do. But guess what? we have the Bible who tells us what God's will is and what we must do. We don't have to wait for God to tell us specifically, in fact He won't tell us, as He has already done that. If we are not willing to do what the Bible tells us to then how can God trust us to do anything, He directly tells us to do.

Luke 6:46-49 (MEV)

46. "Why do you call Me, 'Lord, Lord,' and not do what I say? 47. Whoever comes to Me and hears My words and does them, I will show whom he is like: 48. He is like a man who built a house, and dug deep, and laid the foundation on rock. When the flood arose, the stream beat vehemently against that house, but could not shake it, for it was founded on rock. 49. But he who hears and does not obey is like a man who built a house on the ground without a foundation, against which the stream beat vehemently. Immediately it fell, and the ruin of that house was great."

This portion of scripture is similar to Matthew 7:21-27 but I want you to notice verse 47. Jesus says that whosoever, meaning anyone, who comes to Him, hears His sayings and does them, He will show them who they look like, which is like the wise man who built his house upon the rock.

We can see this clearly in the Wuest version.

Luke 6:46-49 (Wuest)

*But why are you calling me, Lord, Lord, and not doing the things
which I am saying? Everyone who comes to me and is hearing my
words and is putting them into practice, I will show you to whom
he is like. He is like a man who is building a house, who dug and
went deep and laid a foundation upon the solid rock. And a flood
having come, the river dashed against that house, and it was not
strong enough to shake it because it was built securely. But he
who heard and did not do is like a man who built a house upon the
ground without a foundation, against which the river dashed, and
immediately it collapsed, and the ruin of that house was great.
After He ended all His Words in the hearing of the people, He
entered Capernaum.*

We have many instructions on doing the Word. In Luke 6:47 the
Greek word for Doeth is (G4160) poieo- abide, + agree, appoint, X
avenge, +band together, be, bear +bewray, bring (forth), Cast out,
cause, commit, +content, continue, deal, +with out delay, (would)
do (-ing), execute, exercise, fulfil, gain, give, have, hold, X
journeying, keep, +lay wait, +lighten the ship, make, X mean
+none of these things move me, observe, ordain, perform,
provide, +have purged, purpose, put,+ secure, shew, X shoot out,
spend, take, tarry, +Transgress the law, work, yield.

So doing the Word is to abide in the Word, agree with the Word,
exercise, execute;, fulfil the Word, get a hold of the Word, perform
the Word, provide the Word for those that need it; i.e. those that
are sick, shoot out the Word and many more.

What does bewray mean: it's an old English word for reveal. So,
we must reveal the Word of God to people. When we do and
preach the Word we are doing the Word.

Mark 16:15 (MEV)

*15. "He said to them, "Go into all the world, and preach the gospel
to every creature."*

Being a doer of the Word is important. It shows us that we are mature Christian and no longer a babe in Christ.

Chapter 8

Meat Of The Word

As mature Christians, we will no longer need milk but meat. Meat is doing the Bible.

How do we know this?

John 4:6-34 (MEV)

6. Jacob's well was there. Jesus, therefore, being exhausted from His journey, sat down by the well. It was about the sixth hour. 7. A woman of Samaria came there to draw water. Jesus said to her, "Give Me a drink." 8. For His disciples had gone away into the city to buy food. 9. Then the woman of Samaria said to Him, "How is it that You, being a Jew, ask a drink from me, a woman of Samaria?" For Jews have no dealings with Samaritans. 10. Jesus answered her, "If you knew the gift of God, and who it is who is saying to
you, 'Give Me a drink,' you would have asked Him, and He would have given you living water." 11. The woman said to Him, "Sir, You have nothing to draw with, and the well is deep. Where then do You get that living water? 12. Are You greater than our father Jacob, who gave us the well and drank from it himself, along with his sons and his livestock?" 13. Jesus said to her, "Everyone who drinks of this water will thirst again, 14. but whoever drinks of the water that I shall give him will never thirst. Indeed, the water that I shall give him will become in him a well of water springing up into eternal life." 15. The woman said to Him, "Sir, give me this water, so that I will not thirst, nor come here to draw." 16. Jesus said to her, "Go, call your husband, and come here." 17. The woman answered, "I have no husband." Jesus said to her, "You are right in saying, 'I have no husband,'

18. for you have had five husbands, and he whom you now have is not your husband. So you have spoken truthfully." 19. The woman said to Him, "Sir, I perceive that You are a prophet. 20. Our fathers worshipped on this mountain, but you all say that in Jerusalem is the place where men ought to worship." 21. Jesus said to her, "Woman, believe Me, the hour is coming when neither on this mountain nor in Jerusalem will you worship the Father. 22. You worship what you do not know; we know what we worship, for salvation is of the Jews. 23. Yet the hour is coming, and is now here, when the true worshippers will worship the Father in spirit and truth. For the Father seeks such to worship Him. 24. God is Spirit, and those who worship Him must worship Him in spirit and truth." 25. The woman said to Him, "I know that Messiah is coming" (who is called Christ). "When He comes, He will tell us all things." 26. Jesus said to her, "I who speak to you am He." 27. Then His disciples came. They marvelled that He talked with a woman. Yet no one said, "What do You seek?" or, "Why are You talking with her?" 28. The woman then left her water pot, went her way into the city, and said to the men, 29 "Come, see a Man who told me all things that I ever did. Could this be the Christ?" 30. They went out of the city and came to Him. 31. Meanwhile His disciples urged Him, saying, "Rabbi, eat." 32. But He said to them, "I have food to eat of which you do not know." 33. Therefore the disciples said one to another, "Has anyone brought Him anything to eat?" 34. Jesus said to them, "My food is to do the will of Him who sent Me, and to finish His work.

We see that Jesus said that the meat is to do the will of the Father and to finish His work. If we are to be imitators or clones of Jesus, then when we do His will and complete it, then we are doing meat. So what is the will of the Father? The will of the Father is what is said in the Bible. We are to love God with all our heart, soul, and mind. As well as loving our neighbour as ourselves. It's about making earth look like heaven, as it says in the Lord's prayer. How do we love our neighbours? By treating them the same way we would like to be treated. Be there to help them in any way you can, i.e., laying hands on them when they are sick, praying for them every day, if you see a need, you meet it or trust God to help you to meet their need.

Who is your neighbour? Its everyone, including those that hate you.

An idea for helping people in your area. Look at the people that are living in your street and chose the one that gives you the most problems in the street and pray for them every day. Keep a journal of what God is showing you about that person and any changes that happen. You can then add more people in your street and then anyone in your city then anyone in your county or state, then your region then your country, then your world. If you start with one person, and slowly increase it then you will be able to grow your prayer life over more and more people.

John 6:27-28 (MEV)

27. Do not work for the food which perishes, but for that food which endures to eternal life, which the Son of Man will give you. For God the Father has set His seal on Him." 28. Then they asked Him, "What shall we do that we may work the works of God?"

You see the disciples have learnt that when Jesus spoke about meat, He was talking about the works of God

John 6:29 (MEV)

29 Jesus answered them, "This is the work of God, that you believe in Him whom He has sent."

The Works of God (meat) is that we are to believe on him (Jesus), as God has sent him to us to die. We could also say that we need to believe the Holy Spirit as well. Praying and singing in tongues is a great resource we can draw on, not only in times of trouble

but also, in our everyday life. Remember the Holy Spirit is a
person
and is part of the tri-union Godhead. He was sent to guide us into
all truth and be a help.

Paul is writing to the people in Corinthians and he clearly tells
them that they are babes in Christ and he must feed them milk
and not meat, as they were not yet able to manage meat.

1 Corinthians 3:1-3 (MEV)

*1. Brothers, I could not speak to you as to spiritual men, but as to
worldly, even as to babes in Christ. 2. I have fed you with milk and
not with solid food. For to this day you were not able to endure it.
Nor are you able now, 3. for you are still worldly. Since there is
envy, strife, and divisions among you, are you not worldly and
behaving as mere men?*

So, if you are babes or carnally minded then you will only be able
to handle the milk, which is just reading the Word. But if you are a
mature Believer then you can have both the milk (reading the
Word) and meat (doing the Word). You cannot do the Word if you
don't study the Word, and renew your mind, by changing the way
you think about things.

Hebrews 5:11-14 (MEV)

*11. Concerning this we have much to say that is hard to explain,
since you have become hard of hearing. 12. For though by now
you should be teachers, you need someone to teach you again
the first principles of the oracles of God and have come to need
milk rather than solid food. 13. Everyone who lives on milk is
unskilled in the word of righteousness, for he is a baby. 14. But
solid food belongs to those who are mature, for those who through
practice have powers of discernment that are trained to distinguish
good from evil.*

Paul wrote to the Jewish people, telling them that they were not listing to the things that have been spoken about Jesus. In fact, they had become stupid and were not understanding what was being said.

When we are mature then we can eat meat, and we will exercise our senses where we will know what is both good and evil. Note the word exercised, that means doing it. You can't sit in a chair and say that you are exercising, because you are not doing it. So, if we are not reading the Word and doing the Word, we are not growing up to be more like Jesus. If Jesus was doing the will of the Father, which is meat, then we are to do the same because we are to be imitators of Jesus.

1 Corinthians 11:1 (MEV)

1. *"Follow me as I follow Christ."*

To become mature is to do the will and work of God just like Jesus did.

John 4:34. (MEV)

34. *Jesus said to them, "My food is to do the will of Him who sent Me, and to finish His work.*

Who sent Jesus?

Well the obvious answer is God, The Father but we need to prove this by using the Word of God! Never take anything at face value please check it out. This will help you to get the truth.

John 3:16-17 (MEV)

16. "For God so loved the world that He gave His only begotten Son, that whoever believes in Him should not perish, but have eternal life. 17. For God did not send His Son into the world to condemn the world, but that the world through Him might be saved.

In these verses, we not only see that Jesus was God's Son, and a son that God was willing to sacrifice because He loved us so much, that He wanted to have a personal relationship with us. But it also shows that it was God who sent Jesus into the world not to condemn it but to save it.

John 8:28-29 (MEV)

28. So Jesus said to them, "When you lift up the Son of Man, then you will know that I am He, and I do nothing of Myself. But I speak these things as My Father taught Me. 29. He who sent Me is with Me. The Father has not left Me alone, for I always do those things that please Him."

Jesus even tells his disciples that God sent him and that he only did the things that God has taught him.

Galatians 4:4-5 (MEV)

4. But when the fullness of time came, God sent forth His Son, born from a woman, born under the law, 5. to redeem those who were under the law, that we might receive the adoption as sons.

Again, we see at the specific time, or the right time as we would say that God sent his Son to redeem us from the law and that we can become sons of God.

There are many more scriptures that I can pull out for you. But then it does not encourage you to look them up yourself and to learn about who and why Jesus was sent.

Let us look at John 4:35-38, this follows the story of the women at the well, in fact as I read it, it looks like the continuation of the conversation that Jesus was having with his disciples at the well.

John 4:35-38 (MEV)

*35. Do you not say, 'There are yet four months, and then comes the harvest'? Listen! I say to you, lift up your eyes and look at the fields, for they are already white for harvest. 36. He who reaps receives wages, and gathers fruit that leads to eternal life, that both he who sows and he who reaps may rejoice together.
37. For in this is the saying true, 'One sows, and another reaps.'
38. I sent you to reap a crop for which you did not labor. And you have benefited from their labor."*

Here Jesus is talking about doing the Word. We are to pray for people to come and collect the harvest, not pray for people to become the harvest. The harvest is out there, go and collect it. Don't wait for permission from man, you already have it from God.

Doing the Word is the meat of the Word.

Chapter 9

Why Do We Have To Renew Our Minds?

It's a command from God.

Matthew 22:37 (MEV)

37 Jesus said to him, " 'You shall love the Lord your God with all your heart, and with all your soul, and with all your mind.'

If our minds are not focused on God and His Word, then we don't love God with all our minds. This is the first and great commandment. (See Matthew 22:26) This commandment is repeated in Mark 12:30

Mark 12:30 (MEV)

30 You shall love the Lord your God with all your heart, and with all your soul, and with all your mind, and with all your strength.' This is the first commandment.

Let's Look at Mark 12:30 in the Weust.

Mark 12:30 (Weust)

30. and you shall love the Lord your God with your whole heart, and with your whole soul, and with your whole mind, and with your whole strength.

In everything that you do, think, read and act on, if it is not God focused then you do not love God as much as you think you do. Renewing the mind helps you to get to the point where nothing is as important as loving God and loving others.

Acts 17:11 (MEV)

11. These were more noble than those in Thessalonica, for they received the word with all eagerness, daily examining the Scriptures, to find out if these things were so.

Here Luke is telling us that the believers in Berea where more noble that those that where in Thessalonica because they studied the Word of God with all readiness of mind. What worth does the Bible have if we just read it and not change our thoughts and actions to it? It would be just like reading another self-help book on doing exercises and not doing it and wondering why you are not getting fitter.

Paul writes in Romans 7:23

Romans 7:23 (MEV)

23. But I see another law in my members, warring against the law of my mind and bringing me into captivity to the law of sin which is in my members.

Paul is saying that he sees a law that belongs to the members which works to bring him as a captive back into the law of sin. The renewing the mind is so important that if we don't do renew our minds, we can go back into doing the worldly things and not what God tells us to do through His Word.

Romans 7:25 (MEV)

25. I thank God through Jesus Christ our Lord. So then, with my mind, I serve the law of God, but with my flesh, the law of sin.

Our minds can serve the law of God.

Romans 12:2 (MEV)

2 Do not be conformed to this world, but be transformed by the renewing of your mind, that you may prove what is the good and acceptable and perfect will of God.

We see this is a command and the result if we obey that command. We will be transformed when we renew our minds. We will be transformed to be Jesus on this earth.

Renewing our minds will help us to do more of God's will and to get results because we will do things out of habit and will not question if it is God's will to heal the sick, raise the dead, cast out demons, preach the gospel, and make disciples. When we sit down on a chair we don't have to think if it is going to hold us up, we just sit down. That is how the Word of God should be. We see something needs doing and we just do it as it is natural for us to do it.

SUMMARY

WHAT IS RENEWING THE MIND?

It's when you study the Word of God and act upon what you have learnt. Whatever you have learnt be-comes a habit or the norm rather than just a once off. It is a changing of your mind from the way the world thinks to the way God thinks.

WHO HAS TO RENEW THEIR MINDS?

It is not God that has to renew our minds. We are all responsible in renewing our minds to the Word of God.

HOW DO WE RENEW OUR MINDS?

We renew our minds by reading the Bible without religious goggles on and without reading into the scriptures but read the Bible as it is. We also then make declarations out of scriptures so that we can memorize scriptures and it becomes a way of life. Doing the Word also helps to instill what we have read, and also give us experience in the physical workings of the Word. The meat is doing the Word.

WHY DO WE HAVE TO RENEW OUR MINDS?

We renew our minds because God told us too. It helps us to get more results as the Word becomes a habit or the norm. It becomes a natural way of thinking and acting.

www.ingramcontent.com/pod-product-compliance
Lightning Source LLC
Chambersburg PA
CBHW071500150726
48000CB00006B/2655